DISNEY PRINCESS

Look and Find TREASURY

Magical Moments

Illustrated by Jaime Diaz Studios and Art Mawhinney

 publications international, ltd.

Cinderella just loves the dress
her little friends have made
for her! Can you spot some of
their other creations spread
throughout the room?

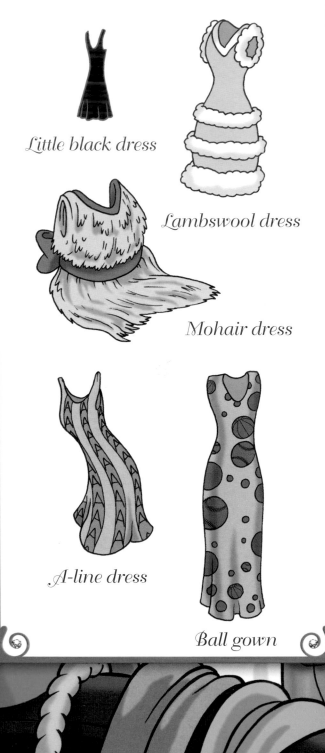

Little black dress

Lambswool dress

Mohair dress

A-line dress

Ball gown

Tiana wants to run her very own restaurant. But for now, she is working toward her dream by waitressing at Duke's Diner. As she heads into work, can you find these examples of New Orleans cuisine on Claiborne Street?

Pecan pie

King cake

Beignets

Pralines

Muffuletta

Crawfish

Jambalaya

Lumiere, Mrs. Potts, and all the other enchanted objects want Belle to feel at home. Among all the snacks and desserts, there are a few unusual things she hasn't seen before. Can you find them?

French bread

Angel food cake

Caesar salad

Chilled asparagus

Strawberry shortcake

Aged cheese

Chicken à la king

Ariel loves exploring sunken ships and searching for treasures from the human world. Now it's your turn to look around. Can you find these fancy fish swimming about the ship?

Crowned cod

Sapphire bluegill

Ruby-red snapper

Goldfish

Silver swordfish

At midnight, Cinderella will lose a glass slipper. But some other maidens at the ball have already lost their accessories! Can you help these ladies find what they have misplaced?

Her earring

Her cape

Her fan

Her necklace

Her glove

Her purse

Tiana and Naveen are human again ... and married! As they prepare to celebrate their happily ever after, look around for these delighted guests.

Louis

Mama Odie

Eudora

Charlotte

Queen

Big Daddy

King

Despite the cold weather, even the birds can't help but notice that Belle is warming up to the Beast. Besides your scarf and mittens, you'll need bird-watching binoculars to find these feathered friends.

Red-headed robin

Hummingbird duet

Love birds

Bald eagle

Bluebird of happiness

Ariel and Eric are married!
It was a celebration like none
ever seen on land or under the
sea! Look at all the friends and
family members who came to
wish Eric and Ariel a happy
ever after.

King
Triton

Carlotta

Scuttle

Grimsby

Chef Louie

Flounder

Sebastian

Max

Explore the worlds of all your favorite Disney princesses as they come alive in these extra busy, extra enchanting adventures. Look for find'ems everywhere from colorful gardens, and charming cottages, to exotic foreign lands!

Look and Find TREASURY

DISNEY PRINCESS

Illustrated by Jaime Diaz Studios

publications international, ltd.

Cinderella

Dear Diary,

The most amazing thing happened today! Just when I thought that I would miss the prince's ball, my Fairy Godmother appeared in the garden. She told me that she would help me get to the ball on time, but that I need to find these unusual things.

A carriage horse

A magic wand

Jaq

This pumpkin

This mouse

This mouse

Gus

Snow White

Oh, Diary!

What a mess! The forest animals led me to a charming cottage tucked away in the woods. It belongs to seven very untidy Dwarfs! I better get to work and start cleaning. Look at all the Dwarfs' belongings that need to be put away.

Grumpy's rocks

Bashful's toy hedgehog

Sneezy's flowers

Sleepy's blanket

Doc's inkwell

Dopey's alarm clock

Happy's chest

Sleeping Beauty

Oh, Diary!

Today is my sixteenth birthday. I am so excited! Not only have I met the man of my dreams, but my forest friends have thrown me a birthday party. Just look and see all the wonderful gifts they have made!

Walking stick

Acorn earrings

Wall plaque

Bracelet

Upside-down cake

Birthday crown

Berry necklace

Jasmine

Dear Diary,

Most people are excited about birthdays, but not me. The law says that I have to marry a prince before my next birthday, but I don't want to. I'm not ready or interested in marrying anyone yet! And you should see some of the characters who have gathered in the palace garden. None of them are my type!

Prince
Ima Stinker

Prince
Abracadabra

Prince Havallama

Prince
Jim Nastic

Prince
Chocolotts

Prince
Nick Nack

Mulan

Dear Diary,

Today I meet the Matchmaker. It's important that I bring honor and dignity to my family. This is such a very special day, but I'm a little late—as always! In all this confusion, I lost a few items. Look around this busy scene and help me gather these things every woman needs.

A pendant for balance

An apple for serenity

This fan

Beads of jade for beauty

Mulan's special comb

A cricket for luck

This parasol

Pocahontas

Dear Diary,

John Smith and I had a beautiful day walking and talking. I wanted to share with him the many valuable lessons I've learned from nature. I think he finally understands. How could he not? The swirling wind is quite a teacher! Look for all these signs of nature to show us how everything is connected and that life is a circle that never ends.

Bear paw

Yellow bird

Butterfly

Shell

Eagle feather

Blue jay feather

Footprint

Welcome to the Enchanted Stables!
Join the Disney princesses and their
trusty steeds as they frolic, trot, and
prance across eight busy scenes.
Hop on board and get in the
hunt for hidden pictures!

Look and Find TREASURY

Enchanted Stables

Illustrated by Art Mawhinney

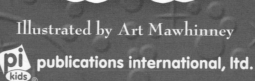

publications international, ltd.

Cinderella and her horse, Frou, are competing in the Royal Horse Show. It looks like Frou is sure to win! Do you see some of the awards he might receive around the horse-show arena?

Blue ribbon

Pink ribbon

Gold medal

Plaque

Wreath

Trophy

Yellow ribbon

Tiana and Naveen are riding in the Mardi Gras parade! Many of the revelers — and horses — are dressed up for the occasion. Can you spot these costumed horses around the celebration?

Mermaid

Jester

Princess

Greek god

Pirate

Genie

Can-can dancer

Aurora and her horse, Buttercup, are visiting Flora, Fauna, and Merryweather. Flora thinks that Buttercup looks best in pink! As the fairies perform their magic, search the garden for these other things Flora turned pink.

Flower

Cake

Cup

Cloak

Hat

Bow

Basket

Jasmine and her horse, Midnight, are racing Aladdin and the Genie. Their course has taken them through the marketplace, where they've managed to cause quite a mess. Look around the stalls for this topsy-turvy merchandise.

This drum

This basket of apples

This cloth

This vase

This pot

These dates

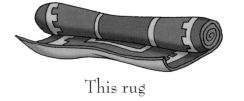

This rug

Ariel is throwing a birthday beach party for her horse, Beau. Many of Prince Eric's loyal subjects have come out to join in the celebration. Do you see these gifts they've brought for the birthday horse?

This present

Saddle

New horseshoes

Basket of treats

This gift box

Brush

Blanket

Snow White and her horse, Astor, are having a picnic with the Prince and the Dwarfs. Their blankets are full of delicious things to eat … and there's plenty for Astor, too! Do you see these foods a horse would especially enjoy?

Apple

Carrots

Bran

Oats

Corn

Sugar cubes

Horse treat

Hay

Mulan and her horse, Khan, are attending a grand Chinese New Year celebration. The village is full of people enjoying the festivities. Can you spot these familiar faces in the happy crowd?

Mulan's parents

Grandmother

The Matchmaker

Shang

Cri-Kee

Ling

Chien-Po

Yao

The Prince has a special surprise for Belle: There's a new baby in the royal stables! Belle wants her new friend to feel at home in the stable. Do you see these special things she has set out for the little foal?

Grooming kit

This basket of carrots

New set of horseshoes

Mane ribbons

Plush blanket

Brush

Gourmet feed

Make a wish and waltz away with your beloved Disney princesses as you watch their dreams come true. Eight enchanted scenes bring all their wishes to life as you look for objects on each page.

BAKERY

Look and Find TREASURY

Wishes & Dreams

Illustrated by Art Mawhinney

pi kids

publications international, ltd.

Tiana's dreams have come true! Welcome to Tiana's Palace, where the food is always hot and the music is smoking. Look for these signature dishes, made by Tiana herself.

Beignets

Gumbo

Braided sweet bread

Crawfish

Red beans and rice

Pecan pie

TIANA

Belle thought she was giving up everything by living in the castle with the Beast, but her life changed beyond her wildest dreams, and made all of her wishes come true! Can you find Belle's favorite stories in this room?

Romeo and Juliet

Thumbelina

Cinderella

Fairy Stories

Sleeping Beauty

The Princess and the Pea

Ariel collects human things from the ocean floor and wishes that one day, she could be part of the human world. Look for these human things Ariel has collected.

Hourglass

Candelabra

Dinglehopper

Box of thingamabobs

This painting

Pair of glasses

Snow White wishes that some day her prince will arrive—and her dreams will finally come true! Until then, she'll use a smile and a song to enjoy each day. Can you find these things that make Snow White smile?

Basket of ribbons

Pot of stew

Flowers

Baby bird

Clean dishes

Gooseberry pie

Rapunzel's wish has come true! She has escaped her tower and arrived in the heart of the nearby kingdom just in time for the lantern festival. Can you find people doing these things that she's been dreaming about?

Riding

Celebrating

Dancing

Splashing

Running

Flying

Sleeping Beauty used to dance with her prince once upon a dream, but now her dream has come true! Can you find her friends dancing at the ball with her?

Birds

Turtles

Rabbits

Squirrels

Chipmunks

Owls

Jasmine always dreamed about adventures outside of the palace walls. Aladdin and his magic carpet have made her dreams come true! Can you find these things that Jasmine has been wishing to see?

Fire-eater

Snake charmer

Human statue

Contortionist

Tightrope walker

Tiger tamer

Cinderella always said that a dream is a wish your heart makes—and her dreams of going to the ball and marrying the prince have come true! Can you find these things at Cinderella's wedding?

Violinist

Bouquet

Gus

Invitation

Bells

Cake

Catch the streetcar back to Claiborne Street and say hello to these people Tiana passed on her way to Duke's Diner.

Take another look at Belle's supper. Can you find these foods from famous sayings?

- A hat with a bite out of it
- A bowl of cherries
- A cool cucumber
- A crumbling cookie
- Spilled milk
- A flat pancake
- A pickle
- Sour grapes

Although most of the animals are assisting Snow White in tidying up the Dwarfs' cottage, a number of them aren't exactly helping. Can you find these animals that are taking a cleaning break?

- One juggling bunny
- Two teeter-tottering friends
- One tightrope walker
- Three jump-roping squirrels
- Two soap-sliding bunnies

Can you spot these musicians who have come to serenade Sleeping Beauty in the forest?

- A mushroom-playing skunk
- A squirrel with maracas
- A bird quartet
- A frog chorus